Nurturing the Leader in your Child

Aditi Chopra

ISBN: 1496103564
ISBN-13: 978-1496103567

ACKNOWLEDGEMENT

I would like to acknowledge Future Leaders of America (members of Lonestar Gaveliers Gavel Club) who have provided their opinions and views on leadership via a survey.

CONTENTS

PREFACE

I remember when I was expecting my daughter, I had a lot of anxiety about how to take care of a newborn. I read every page of the book titled, 'What to expect when you are expecting' and followed it very diligently. The book helped me a great deal in taking care of my newborn. Handling a baby was an unknown phenomenon for me and the book provided the needed security.

My inspiration for writing this book is to give tools to parents who want to nurture a leader in their child. Having held various leadership positions and having written books on soft skills, I want to provide a reliable resource to other parents. Leadership is a complex concept and it becomes even more intricate when as a parent you are trying to groom a leader. When you are mentoring someone you don't have any other relationship except for mentor-protégé, but when you are mentoring your child, the parent in you is more dominant. Speaking from my personal experience, I take every opportunity I get to instill the right skills in my daughter. Hopefully this book will provide a certain level of security to those parents that are seeking answers to leadership questions with respect to their children.

A question that one might ask – Is leadership very different for children as opposed to adults? When I think about it, the answer is not that straightforward. In some ways – yes, it is different but in lot of ways, it is actually quite similar to leadership for adults. When we are nurturing our children, we are teaching them the same skills but in different ways. Our methods are more meaningful and understandable at the age bracket they are in. Sometimes we have to say the same thing multiple times before the child starts to comprehend it. We also train children based on their individual personalities. Every child is different and is unique in his own way.

Children learn a lot in schools but we as parents also play a significant role in shaping their personality. It is very important to teach leadership skills to children at every age so they can become successful leaders as they grow up. They may not recognize and understand everything at a younger age but it is important to sow the seeds. I believe there is a leader in every child; we just need to nurture it.

This book is not a parenting guide, nor is it a tell-all on leadership skills. I will take a very practical approach such that parents are equipped with the right tools to groom their children.

Aditi Chopra

1 LEADERSHIP SKILLS

"The key to successful leadership today is influence, not authority" ~ Kenneth Blanchard

My doctor recently brought up the topic of leadership in relation to providing guidance to her high school kid. She was curious about developing right skills for children during the crucial years of their high school so that they can get selected to the best colleges. This topic has also been brought up when I meet with other parents in and around my daughter's school. But the question is should we think about leadership only when the child is in high school or should we start to nurture these skills early on?

After all, *"Good luck happens when preparedness meets opportunity,"* so why can't we prepare for good leadership?

Developing leadership skills at an early point in your child's life can help ensure that they will have the opportunity to:

• Utilize these skills in college
• Further develop them in their career
• Have a better chance to be a very good, or even a great frontrunner in their chosen profession

Management can be taught in college and business schools but leadership roots have to be deeper than that. It is often debated whether leaders are born or made. But irrespective, my opinion is that children need to be exposed to leadership concepts early on. The more they get exposed to it, the better leaders they become. If we look at some of the influential icons of our time, we will see that their childhood exposure had a great impact on their ability to lead as an adult.

For example, at the young age of thirteen, Bill Gates who was enrolled at an exclusive private school aced every single class they taught. In the eighth grade, Gates took an interest in programming the GE system in BASIC (programming language) and was excused from math to pursue his interest. His interest and exposure led him to write his first computer program: a game of tic-tac-toe that allowed users to play against the computer. And the rest is history.

Steve Jobs spent his childhood in Silicon Valley. He was interested in electronics and gadgets, because he would spend a lot of time in his neighbor's garage, who worked at Hewlett-Packard company. Later on he joined the Hewlett-Packard Explorer Club, where he saw his first computer at the age of 12. He was impressed with the computer and he knew early on that he wanted to work with computers.

Margaret Thatcher, the only woman prime minister of United Kingdom, had her training in early childhood. She helped her father in his grocery business and learned from his interest in local politics. Her school reports showed academic consistency and brilliance in a number of extra-curricular activities.

Definition

Let's first do a level set on what leadership is. When we look at a very simple definition, we often say something trite like this:

"A leader is simply someone who has followers."

But I must disagree with this oversimplification. For instance, I certainly don't consider having 1000 Facebook friends as a sign of leadership simply because of the large number of followers. Sure, someone like this has a lot of "followers" but this doesn't necessarily make them an influencer. On the contrary; I would say that leadership has much more to it than the number of followers one has. And this *follower* fallacy is the case for new leaders, seasoned leaders, and everyone in between.

"Leadership is influence. Nothing more, nothing less." ~Dr. John C. Maxwell

Let's look at some practical scenarios:

• **Initiative**: In this fast paced, competitive world, winning is given a lot of importance. But I always maintain that effort is the most important aspect and should not be neglected. In a competition, not every child can win, but the effort of competing should be recognized. A child who is competing, whether he wins or not is certainly a leader since he has taken the initiative to compete.

• **Consistency:** Consistency is another important quality, be it consistency in getting good grades, dance or music program. Consistency shows devotion and persistence which are good traits to acquire for children.

• **Communication Skills:** Communication skills are crucial for a leader. It would be nearly impossible for a youngster to excel in college interview or admission process without excellent communication skills. Written as well as oral communication skills are extremely important.

• **Personal Strength**: Every leader has some unique quality that sets them apart from others. Leaders can leverage their strengths to accomplish a lot. Children need to figure this strength of theirs and be able to articulate these in their college essays or interviews.

• **Respect**: Children also need to develop self-respect and respect for others. Building self-esteem and self-respect is an absolute must, but it is not enough without the ability to respect others.

Survey Results

I conducted a survey amongst several teenagers to get a pulse on future leaders of America. These teenagers attend the Lonestar Gaveliers Gavel (Toastmasters) club and are already on the path of leadership. They are certainly frontrunners since they have taken the initiative to improve their communication skills by joining the club. Some of them have taken a step further and hold positions such as president or treasurer of the group.

Let's look at some of the findings from the survey.

Attributes: In the survey, I presented these young leaders with a number of attributes. I asked them to identify (according to them) all attributes that are applicable towards leadership.

Attributes	% Responses
Communication	100%
Popularity	30 %
Teamwork	100%
Creativity	80%

Honesty/Integrity	100%
Decision Making	100%
Friendship (Interpersonal Relationships)	90%
Managing Change	90%

Let's take a brief look at results.

Most of the survey takers were able to recognize the relevant attributes. **Managing Change** is certainly a leadership skill which may or may not be obvious to children. Some of them may have developed coping mechanisms to deal with change. For others, they may still be relying on their parents. Regardless, knowing that changes happen in corporations all the time, it is important for leaders to be able to manage change without getting stressed and flustered.

Creativity is another skill that may be very important in certain professions such as entertainment, advertising etc. but may not be crucial in others such as engineering. We have all heard the discussion of left brain versus right brain multiple times. Left brain is associated with analytical thinking whereas right brain is linked with intuitive and creative thinking. Some individuals have a stronger left brain and for others right brain is more active. It is believed that entrepreneurs strongly use both left and right side brain. However, I believe that as parents we should nurture creativity in our children and stimulate that right brain of theirs as well.

Building **Interpersonal relationships** is a crucial leadership skill. The sooner these young leaders develop this skill, the more successful they will become. You will be surprised to know how many adults lack this skill and therefore are sometimes handicapped by it. I have realized throughout my career that many achievements are based on business relationships. Those who understand this and are able to forge strong interpersonal relationships have an easier time navigating their career path.

I was not surprised that very few teenagers selected **popularity** as a leadership attribute. Popularity is a complex phenomenon that teenagers deal with in school irrespective of which part of the world they live and which school they go to. Popularity can be a good thing if a person is widely known because she is helpful to others. A child could also be popular because he is the go-to person for all questions. However if a child is popular because of her looks, that is certainly not a leadership quality. It is important for children to understand the difference. Not every child seeks popularity and for them it is not a crucial thing to have. I will delve into this complex subject in later chapters but it is worth mentioning here.

Quotes: During the survey, I asked these young leaders to define leadership in their own terms. The answers were very inspiring.

"Taking action when needed and helping those in need."

"Leadership is the ability to inspire, engage and influence a group of people."

"Leadership is when you have the ability to take control of a situation and carefully and properly manage your time so that the situation is resolved."

"Making the right choices for people all around you."

"Influence people positively."

"Leadership is the ability to make decisions with the coordinated, cohesive action of a team."

"Leadership is a person's ability to guide others and allowing others to guide as well. It is stepping up to the challenge when no one else does."

"Leadership is not being a follower and standing up for what you believe in regardless of what others think."

"I think leadership is an ability where you are able to be a leader of a group and not making yourself seem like a monarch or tyrant. A strong leader has a strong thought about what's right. Good leadership means that you know how to listen to everyone's ideas and finally coming up with the final resolution. You still have the final say, but you aren't jumping right to it without everyone else."

These future leaders clearly understood the concept and were able to articulate it in their own words. You can also see that each child has his own unique perspective build into the definition.

In following chapters, let's take a look at how parents can nurture all these brilliant assets in their children.

2 EMOTIONAL INTELLIGENCE

"In a very real sense we have two minds, one that thinks and one that feels" — Daniel Goleman

Quite often we identify others' emotions but are oblivious to our own feelings. Sometimes we are not able to relate to others and cannot empathize. These situations are indication of low EQ (Emotional Quotient). Emotional intelligence (EI) is the ability to identify, understand, and manage emotions in a constructive way.

The more we are in tune with our emotions, the more power we have to control them. The more we understand others' emotions, the more effective our interactions become. A high EQ helps us communicate effectively, empathize with others, overcome challenges, and manage conflict. Emotional intelligence impacts many different aspects of our daily life, such as the way we behave and the way we interact with others.

If you have high EQ, you are able to recognize your own emotional state and the emotional states of others, and interact with people in an effective way. You can use this understanding of emotions to relate better to other people and form healthier relationships.

Emotional intelligence consists of following aspects:

- **Self-awareness** – The ability to clearly identify your strength and weaknesses is the key to self-awareness. Some people are naturally highly self-aware and others have blind spots. Until someone points out their weakness, these people may not be aware of them. First reaction on being pointed out a weakness will be to deny it. But the more self-aware you are, the more you will be in tune with your weakness and try to overcome it or at least be aware of its repercussions. A weakness may not always be something you want to work on, but being aware of its existence and impact is a huge step. This gives you great self-confidence.

- **Self-management** – Once you become self-aware, you are more in control of your behavior. Self-management is all about you being able to control any impulsive feelings or behaviors. If circumstances change on you, are you able to handle them without getting all flustered and reacting in an unproductive way? Controlling one's anger in a conflicting situation is an example of self-management.

- **Social awareness** – You are more socially aware when you can understand the emotions, needs, and concerns of other people. People around you will have varying personalities and you don't have control over their biases or behaviors. However, you can control your response to others. High EQ lets you empathize better and pick up on emotional cues from other people.

- **Relationship management** – Finally if you understand your own and other's emotions better, you can develop and maintain good relationships. You will be able to communicate clearly, inspire and influence others, work well in a team, and manage conflict. This aspect will lead you to a healthy and prosperous life.

Why is emotional intelligence (EI) so important?

Intelligence Quotient (IQ) has been talked about a lot. IQ certainly is very helpful for a person. IQ can help one get a degree but what makes a leader more successful is EQ in addition to IQ. As we know, it's not the smartest people that are the most successful or the most fulfilled in life. You probably know people who are academically brilliant and yet are socially inept and unsuccessful at work or in their personal relationships. IQ isn't enough on its own to be successful in life. A high EQ helps you manage stressful situations, conflicts with others and lead a life you have more control over.

Emotional intelligence can help you navigate the social complexities of the workplace, lead and motivate others, and excel in your career. In fact, when it comes to gauging job candidates, many companies now view emotional intelligence as being as important as technical ability and require EQ testing before hiring.

By understanding your emotions and how to control them, you're better able to express how you feel and understand how others are feeling. This allows you to communicate more effectively and forge stronger relationships, both at work and in your personal life.

How to raise your emotional intelligence

Being aware of the concept of emotional intelligence is the first step towards acquiring a high EQ. The next step is to be able to connect to your own emotions and reactions. Using feedback given by peers or by near and dear ones is a very effective way to learn about your emotions. Don't reject if someone is giving you constructive feedback; try to see if there is any truth to it and what can you learn going forward. I listen to feedback carefully, including the feedback given by my daughter.

The key skills of emotional intelligence can be learned by anyone, at any time. There is a difference, however, between learning about emotional intelligence and applying that knowledge to your life. Just because you know you should do something doesn't mean you will—especially when you become overwhelmed by stress, which can hijack your best intentions.

You can take baby steps towards acquiring a high EQ by acknowledging your own emotions and reactions whether they are good or bad. Be open to feedback from others. From time to time, try and seek feedback yourself. If you have gone through some difficult situation in the past, try and analyze it objectively and see how your emotions were at play. Ask yourself if you could have done anything differently if you were more aware of your emotions. You will be surprised by the answer.

I have discussed emotional intelligence briefly in this chapter. In the next few chapters, I will delve into practical application of EI with regards to raising your child and how it can make a difference.

3 UNDERSTANDING YOUR CHILD

"The most dangerous leadership myth is that leaders are born-that there is a genetic factor to leadership. That's nonsense; in fact, the opposite is true. Leaders are made rather than born." —Warren Bennis

It is said that after the child is born, the human brain continues to develop. This development however is significantly dependent on what kind of stimulation it gets. With the right pacing and stimulation, parents can make a difference in the development of their child's brain.

Similarly, I also believe that leadership skills can be developed in a child by providing the right stimulation, nurturing and conducive environment. Schools definitely play a big role in shaping the children but parents have a significant power to shape their child's mind.

Every child is born with a certain temperament or style. This style may or may not be similar to the child's parents. For example, some children are easy to please; some are slow to warm up to strangers and suffer from stranger's anxiety. Some children are shy and some could be difficult. I believe this aspect is not hereditary and could be very different from the parents and/or siblings.

Now that we have understood what emotional intelligence is all about, it is time to understand how it plays a big role in nurturing the leader within your child. If the parent is emotionally intelligent, he (she) can understand the temperament of child easily. Recognizing your child's style is the best thing you can do to nurture his unique personality. It is almost like a mentor-protégé relationship. Mentor is there to help protégé see his potential and grow it. Similarly a parent can play a big role in having his child realize his full potential.

Understanding your child's temperament or style also means that you may have to customize your approach when dealing with your children. The style that worked for one child may or may not work for another and that is completely okay. Your parenting style may be different for a difficult child versus an easy-going child. It is crucial to understand this aspect.

Often we see parents comparing siblings or their children to their friend's children. I was compared to my siblings a countless number of times and I know that it neither helped me nor my siblings. Often parents are heard saying, "But the older one never did that." or "Older one always obeyed me, how come the younger one isn't?" In my opinion, trying to make the same style work for all your children or expecting exactly the same response from them is a very wrong way to approach parenting. It is a sign of parent having a low EQ.

Another disadvantage of comparison between children is that it lowers the self-esteem of the child who is being criticized. Since the child is told that he is not behaving like the other one, he is bound to think that something is wrong with him or that his sibling is better than him. The worst thing you can do as a parent is to mold the child into someone that he is not. Your task as a parent is to understand your child and provide a nurturing environment where he feels safe, happy, encouraged and appreciated.

Self-Esteem

Self-esteem plays a big role in how an adult behaves. People with a healthy self-esteem make great leaders. Their relationship with co-workers and family members are strong and productive. This quality however starts developing at a very early age, much before the child is exposed to school and teachers. Parents therefore play the most significant role in developing self-esteem of a child. Your duty then as a parent is to create a high self-esteem in your child to start with.

For example, if your baby is shy and has stranger's anxiety, it is not the right thing to force him to engage with others in a large group. It is certainly not right to compare him to your friend's child who is happily playing in a group of ten children. Instead, knowing about your child's stranger anxiety, you should start small and slowly introduce him to bigger crowds. You should try and understand what possibly could be the reason for the child's stranger anxiety. Is it because he has not been around children often enough? Has the child been too close to mom and is experiencing separation anxiety. The reasons could be several but how you approach the situation can have a huge impact on your child. When you understand the child and provide a safe environment for him to develop, you develop a trust with the child that is life-long. The last thing you want is your child not to trust you.

Childhood experiences that contribute to healthy self-esteem include being listened to, being spoken to respectfully, receiving appropriate attention and affection and having accomplishments recognized and mistakes or failures acknowledged and accepted. Experiences that contribute to low self-esteem include being harshly criticized, being physically, sexually or emotionally abused, being ignored, ridiculed or teased or being expected to be "perfect" all the time. Many psychologists have researched the correlation of parenting and development of self-esteem. This concept has also been identified as an influential predictor of relevant outcomes, such as academic achievement or adult behavior.

Age appropriate interaction

In addition to understanding your child's temperament, you also need to be aware of which leadership concepts are appropriate at which development stage. Your child's personality will unfold in front of you as he grows up from a baby to toddler to a teenager. If you have a high EQ, you will have an easy time trying to understand your child and help him every step of the way. You will nurture high self-esteem and groom a great leader with integrity and authenticity. I will talk about various aspects in the child's development stage in next few chapters but the key is to be able to understand your child and his growing personality.

Questions to ask yourself:

- What are my child's natural gifts? Am I encouraging them or curbing them?
- Am I subconsciously looking for my own personality traits in my child?
- Am I subconsciously comparing my child to another?
- Am I expecting my child to behave like his sibling?
- Am I helping my child understand his

strengths?

- Am I highlighting my child's weakness or helping him manage it?

4 TODDLER STAGE

"Whenever a toddler sees a pile of blocks, he wants to tear it down." - J. J. Abrams

Let's start with the age where leadership training begins for your child. We have all heard the term *terrible twos*. It is understood to be a very difficult age to manage for all parents. Children at this age are growing in so many aspects, all at the same time. They pick up languages. They start to converse but can't fully comprehend everything. They want to feed themselves but don't completely know how to. They are starting to identify themselves as an individual separate from the parent but are still quite emotionally attached. I believe that leadership training can be introduced starting from this very stage. Let's take a look at different aspects where parents can guide the child.

Linguistic Development

A crucial development at this stage for your child is the language he starts speaking first. It is also the age where children can in fact pick up more than one language if exposed to. As the child grows up, it certainly helps for him to know more than one language; having been exposed to two languages at an early age makes it easier for them to learn more. However, be aware that your child is exposed to the main language that you expect him to converse in at school.

I was talking to an Asian lady who was having trouble with her child at school because the child was not exposed to English at all in the first few years. However, at school she was expected to speak and communicate in English. On the other hand, since my daughter started going to daycare at an early age of one year, she picked up English as her primary language. She was at the daycare eight hours a day, five days in a week and therefore, the very first words she spoke were in English. As a result, she didn't experience any problems communicating in school. In addition, she was exposed to Hindi at home and she picked up Hindi in due time as well. When she started learning Spanish in her elementary school, she found it easier to pick it up, because she already knew two languages.

Learning Environment

As a parent, even at an early age of two years, you need to be aware of what kind of toys, books etc. you choose for your child. Early exposure does set a trend. You need to develop a creative mind in your child starting at this very early stage. I started reading picture books to my daughter when she was four months old. She therefore had a very natural progression towards reading. Puzzles and Legos help in the cognitive development of your child. You need to create the right environment for your child's creative mind to develop. Be it painting or playing with clay, you need to provide a creatively challenging environment for them to learn.

Childcare

For working moms, it is very important to choose a childcare that stimulates your child's brain. Don't just choose a place to park your child from 9a.m. to 5p.m. Instead make sure you spend adequate time choosing the right environment for your child. Ask questions such as -

- does the childcare facility cultivate discipline? What are the cleanliness requirements? Does the caregiver share similar values as yours? Since the child spends a lot of time in the daycare, it is important to find the right environment which is consistent with your own values.

I was very lucky to have found a great caregiver for my daughter when she was one year old. The caregiver had her own set of rules and schedule for the children to follow. My daughter learned a lot about discipline, cleanliness as well social skills by being around other children of varying ages.

Discipline

I believe that a child at this age needs to be handled with lot of care but at the same time discipline is the key leadership skill they learn at this stage. Since the child is learning a lot of different habits and trying to form his own identity separate from the parent, it is important to give them the right direction. If they start to go in the wrong direction, discipline will bring them back on track.

Discipline is the key for all stages of a child but it is important to understand that it starts early and not later. I have seen moms spoiling their child at this age and not enforcing adequate rules. They seem to think that it is too early to discipline and are perhaps heavily influenced by motherly love. But I disagree, a toddler is old enough to understand rules. Habits for discipline have to start early and not later.

I believe that discipline is the very basic requirement for a leader. Only a self-disciplined person can lead a group otherwise it is going to be a chaotic world around him. However the way a parent restraints a child, is the key. You don't want to over or under-discipline. You just have to find the right balance. Keep a good balance between empathy and correction. Even when the child is being controlled, he needs to know that he is well understood and cared for.

You need to also make sure that both parents agree on how to discipline so the child doesn't get confused. When parents disagree in front of the child, it sends a mixed signal. You will be surprised how well children even at this stage can pick up nuances and start to manipulate the parent.

The way you discipline a child affects his self-esteem and how comfortable he feels in being himself in the home environment. I will share a personal story here. My mother was extremely strict and erred on the side of over-discipline. At times, I felt that she perhaps lacked in the empathy aspect. Her first reaction on whatever I did wrong was to punish me. Her punishment was sometimes not proportional to the act. When my daughter was born, I inadvertently started to behave like my mother. However, my daughter gave me feedback (through her actions) which made me reassess my own behavior towards her.

I will cite an example from my personal experience. When my daughter was about two years old, one day, I came back late from work. After I picked up my daughter from daycare, I started to feed her baby food but she was making a mess (very typical of a two-year old). I tried to reason with her for few minutes but since I was tired and stressed, I slapped my daughter on her right cheek. To my surprise, my daughter hit me back right after. I was shocked for a few seconds but I realized that it wasn't her fault. I had in fact, just taught my daughter how to hit. She didn't know that action until I showed it to her and she simply had imitated me. We have often heard the phrase, *Lead by example*; you need to therefore be very cognizant of what you are doing as a parent. After that incident, I never slapped my daughter *ever*. I had learned my lesson. Instead I started disciplining her with timeouts. I got her a timeout chair and things went smoothly after that.

Rules

Another aspect of discipline requires us to set rules for our children. Every parent will have her own rules and they will differ from other parents. But it is important to have rules. Believe it or not, even a two year old can start to understand instructions. In addition, rewards and punishment go hand in hand with discipline. For example, giving timeout to your child is certainly a punishment. On the other hand, getting your child her favorite ice cream is a reward. Use the punishment-reward model to build the sense of discipline in your child.

I will share an example of rules that I had set out for my daughter. I realized early on that when we went shopping, no matter how many stores we went to, my daughter would want to buy something or the other. Very quickly this habit of hers was getting out of hand. Therefore, I sat down with her and explained to her the rule that she can only buy one toy from one store, no matter how many stores we go to. She complained in the beginning but after repeating the same rule a few times, she understood it and then started to choose her only toy amongst the ones she liked in a store. It not only taught her how to follow instructions but also decision making skill. Of course at this age, my daughter didn't know she was learning decision making skills but she certainly exercised that part of the brain.

Based on your child's behavior at this very young age, you will need to formulate your own set of rules and instructions for your child.

Questions to ask yourself:

- Am I over discipling my child?
- Am I not discipling enough?
- Am I using the right means to discipline?
- Have I set rules? Do I have the right tools to enforce rules?
- Is my spouse in agreement with the rules I have set for my child?

5 PRE-SCHOOL YEARS

"A child can ask questions that a wise man cannot answer." ~Author Unknown

You have developed emotional intelligence and are beginning to understand your child's temperament. You have enforced discipline in your child and have already set the ground running by this time. Congratulations! Let's see how you can take this further; let's look at what a preschool age looks like.

A toddler learns by trial and error and you have managed that age well. A preschooler on the other hand, internalizes and processes information. He is very curious and asks a lot of questions. *Why* is a preschooler's favorite word. This is the stage where your child starts to expand his mental capability. Providing a creative and challenging environment at this stage is crucial for their mind to nurture well.

My daughter started going to pre-school and I saw her develop as she was challenged well in school. She got plenty of opportunities to explore her talent in mathematics, art, drama, language, free-play as well as social skills. I realize that not every child goes to pre-school but if they don't, parents have an added responsibility to engage their children in stimulating activities in and outside of home. They should take advantage of community and city events to provide an inspiring environment for their child. Satisfying their curiosity and providing a thought-provoking environment is crucial for this age group.

Discipline

Discipline continues to be an important aspect at this age. You may ask how is discipline different at this age? Children at this age understand cause and effect very well. Therefore it is necessary to enforce a punishment when something goes wrong so it registers in their mind not to repeat the behavior. Punishment could be as simple as taking away one of her privileges. At the same time parents should use rewards to reinforce good behavior. You will be surprised how rewards enforce good behavior at this age. Children learn from cause and effect and gravitate towards the right behavior.

When my daughter was at this stage, I started to give her coins as rewards for her good actions. It helped in multiple ways, she started to understand and count money. It also served as a reward. She would collect enough coins to buy herself a shake or ice-cream of her choice. When she did something wrong or didn't follow instructions, I would take away a coin or two from her collection. This made her sad but she learned cause and effect very well.

Values

This is also the age where children learn values such as honesty, loyalty, frugality and compliance. Parents should take every opportunity to instill the right values starting at this age. Integrity is a skill that all leaders should have. Without integrity a leader will not be able to go far. Such values need to be in your child's DNA.

Leading by example is very necessary to instill the right traits in your child. For example, children at this stage don't completely understand the concept of lying.

They may unknowingly lie to get their way. When that happens, you need to sit down with them and explain why it is wrong to lie. Don't punish them; instead have that important conversation around values. Also as parents you may need to revisit your discipling methods. You need to evaluate if you are being too strict in punishments which might push the child towards hiding and lying. Remember, your preschooler understands cause and effect well. Therefore, you may have to adjust your behavior accordingly.

This is a crucial concept I want every parent to understand. There is a very thin line between over-discipling and the right amount of discipline. When you cross that line, you may inadvertently push your child to start hiding things from you. If that happens, don't be too quick to blame the child, instead take a moment to re-evaluate your methods. In addition, have that open conversation with your child and do a level set.

Social Skills

A preschooler is ready to be taught a lesson or two in social skills. It is better to start early and provide enough opportunities for your child to learn the skill to be social with other children. Even if you are not that social yourself, you want to encourage this skill in your child. In addition, children also start to develop various emotions which they didn't know about before such as envy, embarrassment etc. You need to work with your child if he is envious of another child. If he feels embarrassed in any situation, be there for him. Help him deal with these newfound emotions while he is trying to learn social skills.

A leader is always surrounded by people and has to work with people. Therefore it is quite important for a child to learn how to be with other people if he wants to lead. You will hardly find asocial people make good leaders. They may be visionaries in their own right but will probably not be liked by other people. I am not saying that you have to please others but you definitely need to co-exist and learn the inter-personal skills as early as possible.

I lacked inter-personal skill to start with; my parents are not very social people and I never got a chance to exercise this muscle while growing up. However, when I assumed leadership roles in my organization, I quickly realized that a lot of work was done effectively through business relationships. I therefore had to build this muscle from ground up. If your child has this strength up his sleeve from his early childhood years, it would help him a lot in his career later on.

Teachable moments/Opportunities

I have often seen parents get upset when the child does something wrong, they are looking for someone to blame. They look upon these incidents as undesirable. However, I tend to look upon these episodes as teachable moments or opportunities to develop the right skills in your child. A preschooler is old enough to have a dialogue with around mishaps or undesirable behavior.

It is however very important how you approach the subject. You will have to tackle it without appearing as punitive or passing the blame. Approach it as an opportunity to learn and analyze how we can do things better next time around. Ask your child what lesson he learned and how he would do things differently next time? Offer suggestions and ideas on how to improve. Improvement and learning should be the focus, not what went wrong. For example if your child accidentally breaks a toy, instead of saying "You are in trouble", ask her "What happened to the toy?" Have an open dialogue with your child and try to understand where she is coming from. Their mind is capable of processing this kind of information and they will only benefit from these dialogues.

It is said that leaders learn more from failures than success. The same is true for children. By having an open dialogue with them, you are helping them develop the skill to deal with failure in the right manner.

Questions to ask yourself:

- Are my methods of disciplining my preschooler appropriate or do they need any change?
- Is my preschooler social enough? Can I do something to enhance his social skills?
- Am I spending enough time with my child?
- Am I instilling the right values in my child?
- Is my preschooler's mind challenged enough?

6 ELEMENTARY SCHOOL YEARS

"I think the shyness one feels in childhood is often overcome with time. There are children who hide behind their parents' legs, but you don't see grown-ups hiding behind people. It just doesn't happen. I mean, not that often. People develop social skills over time." - Susan Cain

When your child starts elementary school, it is a proud moment for every parent. You are happy and anxious as well since this is the first time your child is officially starting school. Your young leader is learning a lot at this stage of his life. Let's see how you can provide the needed support.

Managing change

A lot changes in your child's life at this time. She is exposed to the concept of grades and tests. She starts to make more friends at school. She learns a lot more about discipline from school than at home. She deals with different personalities in her teachers. She often has a teacher who is her absolute favorite and perhaps a teacher or two that she doesn't like so much. Your child learns a lot in school, but parents' role is not diminished. In fact on the contrary, parents play a big role in helping their children deal with what happens in school. Starting school is a big change in their life. Children at this age are not equipped to manage change and parents help them deal with it. Parents provide the much needed support at this important stage of their lives.

For example, if the child gets into a conflict with a

friend, she should be able to confide in her parent. Conflict management is not a known skill to them yet. An open dialogue between parents and children help them develop a healthy school life as well. Even if your child doesn't share much about his school life, you need to still talk to him about what happened in school every day and keep that momentum going. You need to give them a safety net so they feel safe to come to you in case they run into problems. Parents also provide the needed encouragement when the child brings home their grades and accomplishments. Parent's encouragement becomes a motivator for the child to perform even better.

Empathy

As children start to grow a little older during their elementary school years, their social skills are still evolving. They are learning how to behave and be around other children. You can help them develop empathy for other children by discussing and giving examples. Empathy is an EQ trait and a leadership skill as well. For example, recently my daughter gave her ice-breaker speech in her toastmasters club. After her speech, one of her fellow club members came up to her and congratulated her on a job well done. It came across to me as a wonderful leadership trait. This child had been trained to have empathy for her school mates and it clearly showed in her behavior. Praising someone for their work or having empathy for a colleague or classmate is a good trait to have. Empathy goes a long way in the corporate world.

Values

Continue to teach values to your children. This is the age where children can very well understand right from wrong. It behooves us as parents to have a healthy exchange of values with our children at this age so that they can discern which qualities of their friends they can emulate and which are off-limits. Whatever things are unacceptable to you, you need to tell them and enforce some rules for them to follow. Have an open-ended conversation daily with your child to learn about their school activities. They will open up and share with you their experiences. These conversations are ideal for enforcing values and also building a bond with your child. As the child turns into a teenager, he will start to go into his own shell and will not share as much information. By that time, you may have lost the opportunity to instill the right values in him.

Summer School Programs

Children stay out of school for a good length of time during summer. I believe that it is not a good idea for their brain to not get exercise during this time. They need to be engaging in intellectual or creative activities during this period. Whatever you choose, make sure your child's brain is challenged well. You may want to choose activities that are quite different from their school such that a different brain muscle gets exercised. The different the exposure, the better learning they get. Take time out to visit museums with your child or engage in different stimulating activities.

Promote self-esteem at home

I have discussed raising self-esteem in your child in various chapters. Let's take a look at couple of sub-concepts. Self-doubt and self-control are two concepts that children need to understand at this stage.

Self-doubt may arise if and when children start

comparing themselves with others. When this happens, as parents you need to reinforce self-esteem and put things in perspective for your children. You need to highlight what unique characteristics your child has and why comparison may not be healthy. Healthy competition is good but it shouldn't lead to self-doubt. Help them choose their path in their own way. Teach them to be comfortable in their own skin and not feel embarrassed about who they are.

However, it is worth mentioning here that parents shouldn't build a false sense of self in their children. That will do more harm than good. When the child goes out in the world on his own, his false sense of self will quickly be deflated and it won't be good for anyone. By false sense of self, I mean don't praise the child unduly. Instead help him develop a healthy sense of self. Help him see his unique strengths and develop them further.

Teaching them self-control is also an important thing at this age. It is very easy for them to lose control at this age and react in an inappropriate manner in case of conflicts with peers. Don't let them develop "My way or the highway approach"; instead teach them self-control. Realize that at this age, it is easier for them to start an action and very difficult to stop it. If the child learns self-control right from the beginning, he will have a high EQ going forward.

Questions to ask yourself:

- Does my child understand different values that I want him to learn and practice?
- How is my child behaving with his friends? Does he display empathy?
- How is my child doing with respect to sharing

resources with other children?
- Does my child have self-control?
- How is my child's self-esteem?

7 TEENAGE YEARS

"The young always have the same problem - how to rebel and conform at the same time. They have now solved this by defying their parents and copying one another." ~Quentin Crisp

Teenage years are probably the toughest for children since they are learning their own individuality and at the same time building lifelong friendships. Their personality is constantly evolving at this age. They have to balance between individualism and the concept of collaboration. They have to find their individuality and yet be somewhat disciplined by their parents. All of this causes a great deal of conflict inside the teenager. If children get a good coach at this stage, they will avoid pitfalls and grow into stable young adults. You want to be that coach for them.

This is the age when children are somewhat lost and keep things from their parents because they are not sure what to share and what not to share. However, I must say that if you did everything right before this stage, this age will not be as difficult to manage. I also think that a high EQ parent will certainly have an easy time managing a teenager. A high EQ parent must have invested a lot of time learning about her child's personality which will start to bear fruit in this delicate age.

Empowerment

The most important lesson I learned for this age group is empowerment. A teenager is old enough to form a strategy or approach of doing things. What I found is that my approach can be very different from my daughter's. There is no right or wrong way of doing things, but it is important for me to recognize that I don't push my method onto my daughter especially at this delicate age. If she had her own process of conducting herself and that brings her success, then I need to recognize and respect that. I need to empower her, let her make her own mistakes and learn from them. It is said that a person achieves the most success when they are in their flow and forcing my course onto her (no matter how helpful it was for me) is going to have a negative effect on my daughter. It wasn't easy at first, but with time, I understood and learned to let go.

On the other hand, if I see her struggling, then the parent in me needs to recognize that and provide her with the appropriate guidance. It is with this delicate balance, that I can nurture the best leader in her.

Popularity

Like I mentioned in Chapter one, popularity is a universal and complex phenomenon that every child has to deal with, especially as a teenager. It is therefore our job as a parent to put it in perspective for them. We need to encourage them to adopt the right behavior and not the wrong behavior simply in order to become popular.

I can understand that for a teenager the urge to be the popular kid on the block is high. But it should be for the right reasons. Whether a child is popular or not, they need to have strong sense of self. They should not start gravitating towards a certain group or behavior simply to conform or to reach popularity. They should understand that it is important to be themselves. Only when a person stays true to themselves, they can thrive. These leaders go a long way. In my survey, I asked the future leaders if they agreed with the statement "A popular person is a leader." They either dis-agreed or strongly dis-agreed. If your child shares a different view, have a conversation with them and put things in perspective.

Friendship

What I have realized is that friendship for a teenager is just about the most important thing in the world. They confide with their friends more than their parents while they are still trying to discover themselves. They are not sure if they should share everything with their parents. They are afraid of being leashed or judged and therefore their friends become their confidants. I don't have any issues with this fact. I have come to terms with it. I do however, believe that company can make a big difference in this impressionable age. I believe that parents need to watch out for their children if their company starts to have the wrong influence. Don't be afraid to intervene if things start to go wrong. For example, on some occasions, they may have conflicts with their friends. Provide an environment where they feel comfortable enough to share their concerns with you. You can guide them if needed. But then again, your job is to offer suggestions and let them handle the situation on their own. It teaches them an important skill called **conflict management**. Conflict management skills will come handy when they start to work in the corporate environment.

Managing Change

Managing change is also a crucial leadership skill. As we know, changes are always happening in corporations and sooner we learn to accept them, the better we are.

These leaders are able to ride the wave and are unharmed by changes. This skill needs to be developed in your child as well. I am not saying that you should create situations just to have them learn the skill but when the situation comes, you can guide them.

Every time the child changes school, he is probably anxious about the change. When your child joined elementary school, you managed the change for him. He was too young to understand the concept of managing change. However you want your teenager to learn this skill and practice it himself. You can guide him by sharing your own inspiring stories or stories of your friends. Help them ease into the new environment without putting any undue pressures. Be there for them as they manage change but let them handle it so they can learn the skill. Tell them that it takes time and they shouldn't expect things to smooth out overnight.

Decision Making

By the time teenagers make it to high school, with the right guidance, they would have already learned quite a bit about their personality. They would have also hopefully made stable friends. As parents, we should strive for finding a balance of power with our children by this age. The focus then is rightfully towards polishing their individual goals. They start to learn how to make decisions on which high school courses to take, which career path to choose for college, which colleges to apply for etc. Parents play a good role here to balance between guiding and letting children develop their decision making skills.

Decision making is a crucial skill for leaders and the sooner the children learn it, the better. Some parents inadvertently make all the decisions for their children thinking that they know best. However, what they don't realize is that their child has not developed decision making skills at all. These children may have a problem making their own decisions in college when they are on their own.

Ways to acquire leadership skills

Your teenager is ready to acquire and practice leadership skills. You should encourage him to find opportunities for acquiring these skills. Let's take a look at some of these avenues.

• **Teamwork**: Participating in school projects, team sports or tournaments is a good exercise in learning the teamwork skills. Team sports dynamics teach children a lot about dealing with different personalities and most importantly about winning and losing. It also teaches them organization skills.

• **Communication**: Speaking opportunities for children such as in speech and debate clubs or Toastmasters club is another way to develop leadership qualities. These clubs can provide skills like thinking on your feet as well as opportunities to learn from each other.

• **Time Management**: If a child is involved in various activities outside of school, one thing they will have to learn for sure is time management. This is a very essential aspect of a successful leader. I see that many adults find it hard to manage their time and more importantly lack the ability to prioritize tasks that they have to work on. Are they tackling the most important tasks first? Are they saying no to activities that are not important in the big scheme of things? Parents can definitely help children develop this aspect by discussing their activities.

• **Volunteering:** Volunteering for different causes is a great way to learn leadership skills. This also teaches them the concept of giving back to the community. Many schools have programs for community work; you can encourage your child to participate. During my survey of future leaders, when I asked them if they agreed with the statement "*I learn a lot about leadership in after-school activities.*" -- they all "strongly agreed".

• **Decision Making**: Parents can also play a big role in developing decision making skills in their children by empowering them in making their own decisions. I let my daughter choose her high school courses but provided the guidance and support as and when needed.

Questions to ask yourself:

- Does my teenager have good company in school?
- Is my teenager involved in different activities outside of school that can enhance his leadership skills?
- How does my teenager deal with popularity concept?
- How does my child feel about making his own decision?
- How is my teenager's self-esteem?

8 SOCIAL MEDIA AND YOUR CHILD

"Social media has given us this idea that we should all have a posse of friends when in reality, if we have one or two really good friends, we are lucky." - Brene Brown

I am a big user and supporter of social media. It has certainly made the world smaller and more reachable. It has given voice to the common person. Social media has also made the reach of businesses easier and wider. Every business, small or large, now has a presence on social media. It is sort of a given that the social media presence is a necessity.

Human Resources department now analyze any incoming candidate through his social media presence. Nearly every professional has a LinkedIn profile that he keeps updated as an on-line resume. The evolution of internet and social media is one of the most powerful as well as impacting invention of modern times. It has become part of our everyday lives. It also begs the question, "How is social media going to impact our children who are the future leaders?"

Would our children be exercising a different muscle than we did growing up? Social media interaction is not a live interaction. The challenges and intricacies of live interaction with peers are very different from those of social media. We exercised a different muscle when we got into a conflict with a friend or peer while growing up. If a conflict arrives in the world of social media, a completely different approach and a completely different muscle will be developed.

I am not saying that live interaction is better than

chatting with friends on the internet, it is just different. I believe as parents we need to ensure our children are getting a balanced interaction with their friends, peers or colleagues. A more balanced interaction will help them hone in on all the skills they need to become great future leaders.

First things first, every social media tool prescribes a minimum age for account holders. As a parent you need to be aware of this minimum age and not let your child open an account earlier than allowed. I have seen various cases where children have opened Facebook accounts before their age allowed it. I don't blame them; I blame the parents for not enforcing the required rules. There is a reason that there is a minimum age because before that they don't have the understanding to use the tool wisely. It is like taking your child to see an R rated movie. It is not the fault of the movie maker, it is your fault for not seeing the rating. I can understand the curiosity but parents should be aware of how and when their children are using various social media tools.

If you are not into social media, perhaps you should learn a thing or two so that you know what your child is getting into. There are new social media tools being launched every now and then. Teenagers like to follow the trend and will quickly jump onto adopt the latest and greatest. Have a discussion with them around their favorite social media tool. I asked my daughter to help me open my Instagram account. It helped us connect on this common tool that teenagers use these days and I also learned how she was using it. I could then decide if her usage was safe or not. The reality is that social media is not going away. Future leaders will be using social media to communicate. But as parents we need to ensure that our children use it wisely and safely. You can look into who do they have as contacts in their social media tool. Ensure that their profile is private and not open to public. They may have inadvertently not set the right privacy settings and you can help them with that.

Social media can be used for learning as well. Encourage your child to learn about current events by usage of their favorite tool. They are going to use social media tools anyway, might as well help them use them properly.

Questions to ask yourself:

- Is my child over-exposed to social media?
- Is my child using social media avenues in the right and safe manner?
- Does my child spend too much time on social media? Is it becoming a distraction?

9 LEAD BY EXAMPLE

"Before you are a leader, success is all about growing yourself. When you become a leader, success is all about growing others." —Jack Welch

Finally, I will advocate for parents to lead by example in front of their children. No matter how well you train your children and teach them values and skills, what they pick on a lot from is how you behave. You as a parent are the best teacher or mentor for your children and therefore you need to exhibit all the appropriate skills you want your children to acquire. During my survey of future leaders, when I asked them if they agreed with the statement "*I learn about leadership by observing others.*" -- they all "strongly agreed".

When I was growing up, I learned a lot from the way my father carried himself. I remember him teaching me about values and discipline when I was very young. I still remember some of his teachings. I may not have realized it but subconsciously I was learning to be like him. I have always been devoted to my work because I saw my father absolutely worshipping work. I couldn't imagine being any other way.

Think about what you are doing to engage your own children in the conversation of leading others effectively. What are you doing to support an environment where discussions of leadership are encouraged and maintained? How are you impacting the lives of young people by being a role model yourself? Do you share your own personal stories that advocate leadership? Do you share stories of others that exemplify traits that are important?

Parents can also cultivate the right skills in their children by having a conversation around role models. Growing up, I was deeply inspired by a well-known Indian freedom fighter, Mahatma Gandhi. As my daughter was growing up, I would often tell her stories about Gandhi, and encouraged her to tell me who her role model was. I would also tell her why and how Gandhi impressed me and which qualities of his I wanted to acquire. A fruitful conversation around role models and their characteristics can inspire the right thinking amongst your children.

Survey Results

During my survey of future leaders of America, I asked them who their favorite leader was and what they liked about them. Let's look at some of the answers I received.

"My parents, because they have helped me my whole lifetime and they will always be there through thick and thin. I am who I am thanks to them."

"Marissa Mayer, because I can identify with her previous struggles and challenges."

"I think Gandhi was a great leader because he showed that you can do whatever you want no matter what as long as you strongly believe in what you are doing."

"Abraham Lincoln. He was able to help the nation survive despite all the terrible events that occurred during his presidency."

"*My favorite leader is Mahatma Gandhi because he didn't care about what others thought and what the popular path was. He took what he felt was most beneficial for the cause he worked for and that is a true leader.*"

"Martin Luther King Jr. because he stood up for what he believed in and wasn't a follower."

"I think my favorite leader is Abraham Lincoln. He ran for president and, right before the Civil War, had one decision in mind: to abolish slavery. The North and South disputed over slavery, and, with his thoughts as well as the North's, it was abolished by the Emancipation Proclamation. This act is one of the reasons why the United States is how it is today."

As you can see from the quotes, these children grasp a lot from their heroes. It is important to discuss role models and help children learn about successful leaders.

Be The Mentor

I have discussed various concepts in this book in order to provide parents with the right set of tools to nurture leadership within their child. I also tend to think of parent as a mentor. Just like you would mentor someone at work, you can mentor your child and develop his strengths. Mentoring comes with a lot of responsibility and requires patience and passion. The mentor needs to provide a safe and comfortable environment for the protégé and allow him time to develop the right skills. A conventional mentoring may be short-term but when you mentor your child, it is a long-term commitment and comes with a great responsibility.

Take time to mentor your child and help him recognize his strengths. When he does something extraordinary but doesn't completely comprehend it, break it down for him and tell him why it was so profound. Give him examples of how great leaders have done something similar.

In addition to developing your child's strengths, if you notice any weaknesses, it is also your responsibility to make them aware of it in a constructive way and help them manage it. Teach them to play on their strengths and not let their weaknesses come in the way. It is important for them to understand that every person has strengths and weakness but leaders succeed by playing on their strengths!

Questions to ask yourself:

• Am I exemplifying leadership in front of my children?

• Am I exhibiting the right values that I want my children to adopt?

• Am I telling my children to behave in a certain way and not following it myself?

ABOUT THE AUTHOR

Aditi Chopra is a seasoned leader in the software industry. She has a passion for helping people succeed in their careers and is motivated to share her knowledge through her books. Her readers get practical take-aways that they can utilize in their career.

She has authored three popular books on leadership skills titled "Ten Mistakes A Manager Should Avoid", "Leading Without Authority" and "Leaders Turn Crisis Into Opportunities".